# One Sided Love Affair

*One-Sided Love Affair*
Copyright © 2016 Sheryl Walcott

This is a work of fiction, and no part of the
book or any illustrations may be used, except for
brief excerpts in a review, without written permission from

Clay Jars Publishing
2152 Ralph Avenue #414
Brooklyn, NY 11234
http://www.clayjarspublishing.com

Illustrations copyright © 2016 held by
Clay Jars Publishing

The author can be reached via email at:
sherylwalcott@gmail.com

Library of Congress Control Number: 2014943164
ISBN-13: 978-0-9843369-3-7

Some of the Scripture texts in this work are taken from Holy Bible, New International Version®, NIV® Copyright © 1973, 1978, 1984, 2011 by Biblica, Inc.® Used by permission. All rights reserved worldwide, Some "Scripture taken from The Message. Copyright © 1993, 1994, 1995, 1996, 2000, 2001, 2002. Used by permission of NavPress Publishing Group." Some "Scripture taken from the NEW AMERICAN STANDARD BIBLE®, Copyright © 1960, 1962, 1963, 1968, 1971, 1972, 1973, 1975, 1977, 1995 by The Lockman Foundation. Used by permission." Some Scripture taken from Berean Study Bible (BSB) © 2016 by Bible Hub and Berean. Bible. Used by Permission. Any quotation marked AP is the author's paraphrase.

## DEDICATION

### ***Ode to My Heavenly Father***

*Never thought I'd be on this journey
Yet here I am
It's you, my Heavenly Father
who saw it all along
To you be all the Glory and Praise.*

*You saw in me that which I didn't see.
I lift you up all my days
And like David said:*

*"One thing I ask of the Lord, this is what I seek:
That I may dwell in the house of the Lord
All the days of my life,
To gaze upon the beauty of the Lord
And to seek Him in His temple."
Psalm 27:4 (AP)*

*I thank you for being
In and on this
Journey
For unless you are in, it's all in vain.
Father, I thank you for taking me on this
Journey.*

*Thank you for not giving up on me
Thank you for the people you have
Brought into my life,
Who encouraged me every step of this journey.
Thanks for how much I've grown.
Thanks for how much I've learned.
Thank you for YOU.*

*DEDICATION*

**To my Mom, Eugenie**

*MOTHER*
*Unique to the family*
*You've been given*
*You've endured the*
*Pain of labor*
*And labored in pain*
*To provide the best*
*As we face the tests*
*On the journey planned for us.*

*MOTHER*
*Sacrificially planting your*
*Unconditional love*
*Through uncertainty, hard work, tears, fears*
*You are the vessel God chose*
*To knit and form us in your incubator*
*We are connected forever*
*By that cord*
*From which flows your DNA:*
*Kindness*
*Soft heart*
*Selflessness*

*MOTHER*
*You are a gift, blessed and highly*
*favored and flavored by God.*

*DEDICATION*

**To my Sister, Marie**

*Life was breathed into our body
and brought to mine
Instantly we united
Thankful you were
Through the rough and the good
Thankful you are
On this journey we've set forth to master, overcome, conquer
In you lies a sea of worth and value:
Compassionate
Selfless
Considerate
Kind
Giving
Loving
Gentle
Strong
Faithful
Full of Integrity
Your heart Oh
Of flesh and not of stone
Toiling through the night to achieve
How you turn music into inspiration
All flock to you, sweet as the dew
when the rain is wet
Fun, Bubbly, Risk-taker.
Putting aside self for the sake of another
With you I've learned much...
Muchas gracias, mi Hermana!*

*DEDICATION*

**To my Big Sister, Monica**

*Always wanted a big Sis*
*And then we found you*
*From the day we met*
*The pride in me rose*
*You were the first*
*To wet my tongue*
*With the appetite to dream Big*
*Wish you were here to see this dream Fulfilled*
*Big Sis,*
*You are*
*Gone, but not forgotten.*

*Epigraph*

*"Love is an act of the will, never the emotion."*
*-Reverend A. R. Bernard*

*"Never accept your emotions as evidence of truth. Godly wisdom is built on truth. Human wisdom is built on sentiment."*
*-Reverend A. R. Bernard*

*Do not arouse or awaken love until it so desires.*
*(Song of Songs 8:4 - NIV)*

## CONTENTS

*The Poet's Inspiration* ................................................. 1

*Introduction* ............................................................... 5

*Prologue* .................................................................... 6

*Wrestling Within* ....................................................... 7

*THE ONE* ................................................................. 12

*Heat* .......................................................................... 15

*What's Within?* ......................................................... 17

*Our Kiss* .................................................................... 20

*No Words, No Commitment* ..................................... 23

*Questions* .................................................................. 26

*One-Sided* ................................................................. 29

*I Wish I Didn't Like Him* .......................................... 31

| | |
|---|---:|
| *PAIN* | 34 |
| *Anti-Ode to Happiness* | 36 |
| *Three Hundred and Sixty-Five* | 39 |
| *This Scar I Have* | 42 |
| *LOVE* | 45 |
| *Epilogue* | 50 |

*THE POET'S INSPIRATION*

*From the day God revealed to me He had a plan and
a purpose for my life it was on and I knew
NO HUMAN COULD TAKE THAT AWAY
FROM ME!
Thank you, Heavenly Father!!!*

*Jeremiah 29:11 (NIV)
For I know the plans I have for you,
declares the Lord.
Plans to prosper you and not to harm you.
Plans to give you hope and a future.*


*God says there is nothing we can plan to do
that will be impossible.*

*Philippians 4:13 (BSB)
I can do all things through Christ who gives me strength.*

*THE POET'S INSPIRATION*

**Ode to Poetry**

*Where were you all my life?*
*Never thought I could express you*
*So our relationship was intensely one-sided*
*Day and night*

*Night and day*
*We did nothing but rhymes*
*And more rhymes*
*Until we were exhausted*
*How many times did we do?*
*The cat sat on a mat*
*With a hat and ate a rat*
*We wore that one out*

*You implore us to*
*IMAGINE*
*Perceive*
*Explore*
*Rethink*
*Dig deep*
*Be accountable*

*Everyone has you*
*But only a few discover*
*And become conscious*

*You are vivid*
*You are pieces of me*
*You came years ago*
*But I discovered you late*
*Now our relationship is filled*
*With the new.*
*Flowing through*

*Sassy Sestinas*
*Sing song Sonnets*
*Explosive Ekphrastic*
*Awkward Alliterations*
*Enjoyable Enjambments*
*Rowdy Rants*
*Outrageous Odes*
*Apathetic Apostrophes*
*Moody metaphors*
*Acoustic Acrostics*
*Simmering Similes*

*What an exciting adventure!*

*Thank you for allowing me on this journey*
*To release all that's within*
*I used to hear of you but now*
*I know you*
*I taste you*
*Keep stirring within me, Poetry*
*Keep stirring and let my cup overflow*
*With the goodness that comes from you.*

## *INTRODUCTION*

*1 Corinthians 13: 4-7 (NIV)*

*Love is patient,*
*Love is kind.*
*It does not envy,*
*It does not boast,*
*It is not proud.*
*It does not dishonor others,*
*It is not self-seeking,*
*It is not easily angered,*
*It keeps no record of wrongs.*
*Love does not delight in evil but rejoices with the truth.*
*It always protects, always trusts, always hopes,*
*always perseveres.*

*PROLOGUE*

*A girl ventures out on her perception of a "love affair" only to realize that it's one-sided. The path she travels takes her through emotional peaks and valleys to the mountainous place of redemption, declaration of self, and a healthy vision of love. This is her journey...*

## Wrestling Within

A war was always raging inside. She's always been career-minded with love at the back of her mind, or so she would like most to think, including self. Should she remain focused on what she knows will not abandon her or should she finally open up and allow love to enter in without the fear of abandonment? After all, she didn't want to be hurt. Seen too many hurt...

*WRESTLING WITHIN*

*Smitten, let me say this:*
*Don't need a man*
*Things to accomplish in life*
*Don't need a man*
*To slow me down*
*Don't need love*
*I've got it when the work's complete*
*Though*
*It would be nice*
*A family*
*A life...*
*HEY!*
*FOCUS!*
*Deadlines await*
*Love halts things*
*Focus on what matters*

*Independent, I hear you*
*But*
*I totally want to*
*Meet love*
*I totally want to*

*Touch love*
*Sure sometimes I'm in the clouds*
*And probably should get busy*
*fulfilling*
*What I was placed here to be*
*HEY!*
*FOCUS!*
*Don't need to spend my time busy*
*bustling*
*Watching days go by*
*As I grow ancient.*

*Smitten, love your round table talk*
*But*
*Where are the true loves?*
*Where are the endlessly faithful?*
*Where are the forevers?*

*Work*
*Never fails*
*Work*
*Always fulfills*
*Work*
*Wants to be with me*

*Independent, don't know the answers*

*But I too have some questions*
*Does work hold you?*
*Does work talk to you?*
*Does work really stay with <u>you,</u>*
*forever?*

*Love*
*Give it a try*
*Love*
*You've got to be vulnerable*
*Love*
*Wants to be with you.*

*Smitten,*

*Yes Independent,*

*I lied*
*I want what you've got*

*Independent,*

*Yes Smitten,*

*<u>I</u> lied*
*I want what you've got.*

## The One

Have you ever been attracted to two people? She was. One on whom she'd laid eyes when the journey began with her Lord; let's call him Chocolate. He ministered a song she will never forget. She was drawn to his ministry and of course him. But, he was out of her league. There was no way he would ever have communicated with her. So she thought. The other, she laid eyes on while traveling to work; let's call him Caramel. A conversation was started and... Since Chocolate was out of her league, she decided to give Caramel a try. "How many times must great guys come and go without you giving one a chance?" she asked herself. And so the door was ajar.

*THE ONE*

*I don't know...*
*I don't know which one of the two is*
*The one*
*I thought my mind was made up about*
*The one*
*With his caramel charm*
*But now The other confident*
*With his chocolate grace*
*Is back in the picture*
*So now I don't know.*

*I don't know which of the two is*
*The one*
*Heaven look down on my dilemma*
*And help me to know*
*For I don't know...*

*I don't know who truly cares for me*
*I don't know who will pursue me*
*I don't know who wants*
*To get to know me*
*I don't know who wants*
*To share their life with me*
*I don't know who wants to marry me*
*I don't know which of the two*
*God has for me.*

## The One

*In the end it will come down to this...*
*Who is willing to be transparent*
*With me?*
*I don't know.*

### Heat

She was still unsure of whom, until the power of touch, or so she thought...

*HEAT*

*His hands touched mine*
*Electricity surged*
*I felt a heat I could not explain*
*A heat born not of lust*
*But hot enough to make me take*
*Notice*
*What was that?*
*Was the immediate question*
*As my brain went through*
*Files that would explain,*
*Only to come up empty*
*My heart, filled with emotions*
*Was on a Rollercoaster Ride*
*Did he feel it too?*
*Oh, he must have...*
*Can't sleep.*
*Oh God what's going on?*
*Please help me to settle this so I*
*Can ease away to Sleepy Land*
*Throughout this time the heat*
*Remained...*
*It's no use unable to shake it*
*Just ask him!*
*Oh I will!*
*As sleep came, the heat like a candle lit*
*Refuses to be dimmed.*

What's Within?

This guy had been hurt before and was hard to crack.
Sure he shared some, but always held back...

*WHAT'S WITHIN?*

*He feels the pain
Down deep within
But refuses to share
What's within?*

*The pain of his past
Reflects in his relations
Yet he refuses to
Go within.*

*Hurtful things in times past
Are buried in the innermost
Forever?
Oh dear God no!*

*What will it take?
Who will it take?
To draw it out!
Heaven give me wisdom
How to go about
Pulling it out.*

*And then lightning
Revelation came
TRUST
PATIENCE
LISTENING
MUCH LISTENING
Is what it will take*

## What's Within?

*To draw from within him*
*What will come forth*
*Like a breaking dam.*

## Our Kiss

Enough was shared to cause imagination to go wild. He led her to believe that they could be. What would it be like to kiss him?

*OUR KISS*

*Oh I look forward to that day,*
*That moment in time*
*When we will be given the chance*
*To merge ourselves*
*In each other and lose self,*
*Don't know where it will be or*
*When it will happen.*

*I imagine it to be one that will be full*
*Of exploding Passion and heat*
*A moment we won't want to end*
*It will be sweet, tender, soft and hard*
*One that will be difficult to shake*
*Even after it ends*
*In that kiss we will realize that we are*
*For each other.*

*Contained emotions will explode*
*Spirit and body*
*Will war against each other*
*For within we will burn with*
*The heat of passion*
*That will cause our loins*
*To become aflame*
*So much so that we will*
*Desire to love on each other*
*Through the intertwining of our bodies...*

## Our Kiss

*Skin on skin*
*Sweat on sweat*
*For we together in ecstasy will be*
*A heat so great no sun can give off*
*But that's not to be*
*At least not just yet...*

*So we will look deep into each other*
*Through the windows of our soul and separate reluctantly*
*To our humble abodes*
*Where we will relive over and over in our being*
*Our kiss.*

NO Words, NO Commitment

She waited patiently for him to say this would go somewhere, but...

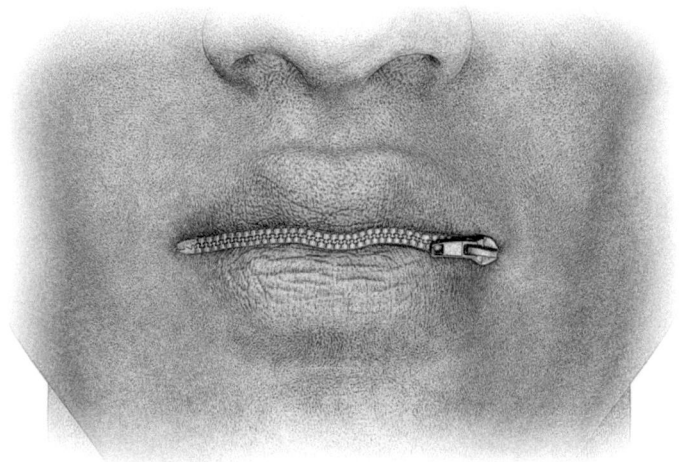

*NO WORDS, NO COMMITMENT*

*He never said a word*
*One way or another*
*And so I was left*
*Standing in the middle.*

*Trying to decipher*
*Which can be a deadly thing*
*Especially when assumption steps in.*

*If he said a word*
*One way or another*
*Commitment would make him eat*
*His words,*
*Hope would raise her beautiful head*
*So I guess things are best left*
*Unsaid.*

*Or should it?*
*For when not a word is said*
*Thoughts are tossed to and fro*
*Which too can be a deadly thing.*

## No Words, No Commitment

*In the midst of all this*
*Expression will share too much*
*And make a fool of herself*
*In her quest to be transparent*
*Which can be a deadly thing.*

*Throughout all these internal things...*
*He never said a word.*

## Questions

Having never been in love and feeling the way she was, questions floated...

*QUESTIONS*

*Am I in love?*
*If this is what love is?*
***I DON'T WANT IT!***
*Should love hurt like this?*
*Should love make you struggle with yourself?*
*Tell me please.*

*Shouldn't love make you float*
*On cloud 9?*

*Can't stop thinking about him.*
*Am I crazy?*
*Tell me please.*

*Love, oh love*
*Where are you?*
*I can't find you.*
*Don't you want me?*
*Tell me please.*

*Oh, the pain.*
*Make it go away!*

*Is something wrong with me?*
*Maybe I'm wrong for you.*

## Questions

*Oh, my love*
*Tell me please.*

*Should I step aside*
*And wait*
*For another?*
*Tell me, please.*

## One-Sided

Reality hit like a barreling train. How stupid of her to think it was going the way <u>she wanted.</u>

*ONE-SIDED*

*It was all in my head though,*
*I allowed it to penetrate my heart*
*What?*
*The thought that he could,*
*Really open his heart to,*
*Let a person like me in*
*To give love another chance.*
*But it was all in my head*
*And now in my heart*

*What must I do now?*
*To rid myself of these emotions*
*My head told me that*
*He was interested*
*And my heart leaped with excitement.*
*Finally!*
*I've allowed myself to be*
*Vulnerable enough for love*
*To open the door left ajar.*
*But it was in my head*
*And now my heart*

*Oh God, help me to flush*
*My system of these false thoughts*
*Cause it's all in my head*
*And now my heart*

I Wish I Didn't Like Him

Is this happening? He said he was not ready for a relationship, but still was leading her on. Why pretend to others that something is? Why not say something?

*I WISH I DIDN'T LIKE HIM*

*I wish I didn't like him*
*But I do*
*For then I wouldn't feel the way I do*
*I wish I didn't like him*
*But I do*
*For then I wouldn't feel the need*
*To want to speak to him*
*But I do*

*I wish I didn't like him*
*For then things wouldn't be this way*
*But it is*
*I have never felt this way before about Anyone like I do him*
*But I do*

*I wish my heart didn't ache the way*
*It does*
*But it is*
*Lord, what must I do to change*
*This feeling*
*I feel in my heart for him?*
*FOR I NEED TO…*
*I HAVE TO…*
*Oh please show me the way!*
*I wish he would tell me to "get lost"*

*But he's not*
*And so the feeling for him is hot.*

*It's this feeling that I feel*
*Why I do these "crazy" things*
*Oh, I "hate" that I feel this way for him!!!*

*I WISH I DIDN'T LIKE HIM!*
*I WISH I DIDN'T LIKE HIM!*
*I WISH I DIDN'T LIKE HIM!*
*Oh, but yet I do.*

### PAIN

The very thing she was afraid of happened. Hurt. She had seen many people hurt and certainly didn't want this for herself, hence the focus on her work. This is what happens when you give love a try.

*PAIN*

*Pain, it hurts so much*
*Pain, it shows so much*
*Pain, it reveals so much*
*Pain, it hinders a lot*
*Pain, it hardens the heart*
*Pain, will cause the tree of bitterness to*
    *grow*
*Pain, produces fear*
*Pain, causes questions to formulate*
*Pain, will it happen again?*
*Pain, how can I trust anyone?*
*Pain, causes you to pull back,*
    *Like a turtle retreats inside his shell*
*P-A-I-N*

## Anti-Ode to Happiness

Sadness covered like never before. It pulled her deep down. Tears flowed and flowed as her heart ached. How stupid was she? What awful decisions she made.

*ANTI-ODE TO HAPPINESS*

*Happiness,*
*You are not welcome here.*
*For today,*
*I want to remain sad.*

*Today,*
*I want to wallow in this murky*
*Water of gloom.*

*Don't you dare come around!*
*Let me be!*

*I see you,*
*With your*
*Energy*
*Smile*
*And perky ways*

*Go away!*
*Get away!*

*As far as one's eyes can see.*

*Can't you see you are not wanted today?*
*What's that?*
*Oh really?*

*What makes you think?*
*I need you*
*Today*

*And*
*That*
*I need to forget*
*That which*
*Has been done to me?*
*Today*

*Please, I beg you,*
*Go back into that Abyss*
*Today.*

## Three Hundred and Sixty-Five

Life revolves around 365, filled with ups and downs. One ends but another comes with promise.

## *THREE HUNDRED AND SIXTY-FIVE*

*Rainy days, cloudy days*
*Wet days, grey days*
*Fun days, Sundays*
*Paydays, Fridays*
*Sunny days, bright days*
*Light days, quiet days*
*Dark days*
*Hair days Bad days, good days*
*Happy days, sad days*
*Boring days*
*Busy days*
*Lazy days*
*Holidays*
*Sick days*
*Wedding days*
*Birthdays*
*Church days*
*School days, Study days*
*Work days, Mondays*
*Two days*
*Thirty days*
*Vacation days*
*Movie days*

# Three Hundred and Sixty-Five

*Young days, shallow days, party days,*
*Modern days*
*Old days, wise days, ancient days,*
*Latter days*
*Shopping days*
*Long days, short days*
*Laundry days, cleaning days*
*Summer days, hot days, not days,*
*Beach days*
*Winter days, cold days, clothes days*
*Today's*
*End of days*
*New days.*

## This Scar I Have

She is slowly coming out of the funk. Days are looking brighter. As she reflects, she recognizes and realizes how she got here... Her own stupidity... Her own wants and desires. She wanted love so badly. But the One True love was always in the wings, waiting to rescue.

*THIS SCAR I HAVE*

*This scar I have...wanted to break me.*
*I remembered when it first entered*
*My life.*
*I didn't ask for it*
*But like some who choose to come*
*By force*
*Violently it came.*
*My world spiraled into negativity.*
*I thought I was insane*
*I tried to be invisible but to no avail.*
*Society second-guessed me*
*What kind of girl is she?*
*For scars are reserved for bad girls*
*And a bad girl she was not.*

*I must confess for a time it had me*
*In its dirty little world*
*Filled with doubt and un-surety*
*I didn't think I'd get out...*
*Until the hand from Heaven*
*Reached out and took my spout*
*Today, with all my being*
*I can safely say I'm out*
*And now the scar that had me*

*No longer can claim clout.*
*For I declare I have it*
*By its sneaky snout*

> **ALL GLORY BE TO HEAVEN...**
> **FOR NOW I'M STANDING**
> **STOUT!**

## LOVE

How can she love someone if she doesn't love herself first? How can she treat others the way she wants to be treated if she doesn't treat herself right? She stopped the insanity long enough to ask, what is love? To THE BOOK she went. THE BOOK she'd put aside to carry out her endeavors. 1 Corinthians 13 to be exact, and there it was. She declared that no one can truly love unless they know the Father. He is Love. She declared that no man can truly love her unless he loves the Father. Love is reciprocated. When a man loves a woman, he goes after her. When love comes both will know. After all, God had removed from him and placed in her something that he needs, and there is something in him that she needs. Together they become one before God and before His eyes they are whole. Love happens at the right time. A process of maturity must take place before the two can become one. She declared that she would wait while God works on her just as He is working on the one. She also declared that if love didn't come, she would be content where she was. After all, fulfilling her life's purposes was most important. She wants to double the talents she has been given, and hear Him say, "Well done thou good and faithful servant."

LOVE

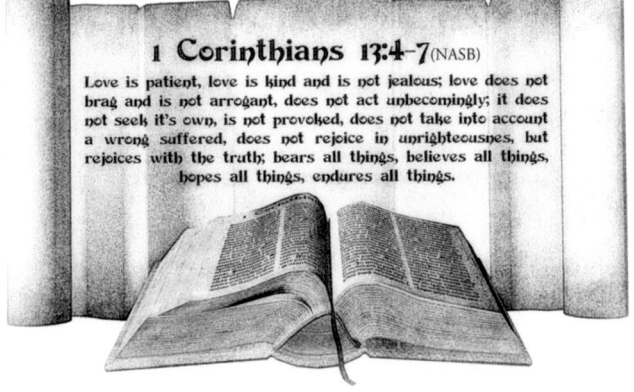

*LOVE*

*I desire to be in love with you*
*To share with you*
*My being, my body, Soul and Spirit*
*When will you break free from your*
*Boundaries and come join me my love?*
*I wait in eager expectation*
*Of your visit to my humble abode*
*I will love you not as the world claims*
*Love to be*
*But as God who is Love says love is.*

*My love, I promise*
*To be patient with you*
*My love, I promise never to hurt you, for I*
*desire to benefit you at my expense*
*My desire is to be with you, to love you, to*
*feel you, to need you.*
*My heart is open and vulnerable*
*To receive all of you,*
*With your flaws and imperfections*
*Come now my love, my heart is pounding*
*with the excitement of being with you.*

*My love, with you in my life,*
*We together will be one.*
*One in purpose, mind, thoughts and actions.*

*Together we will go about*
*Our Father's business and fulfill*
*Our missions set in place by God*
*Before the world began.*

*My love, don't be afraid to remove your*
*armor and come by to be set free indeed by this vastness*
*of love that awaits you.*

*My love, all these things I will do for you*
*I want you to do for me.*
*When we finally meet, my love*
*We will say, what took us so long*
*To find each other?*
*Oh, but I know why my love, it's because*
*Our Father wants us*
*To be ready for each other*
*So that there are no obstacles*
*Within and without to hold us back.*

# Love

*My love, as the years go by*
*When we are together*
*I promise to support you through*
*Thick and thin*
*And we will smile at each other*
*Day by day*
*Until that time comes when our Father*
*bids us come home,*
*My love.*

*EPILOGUE*

*Lessons She Learned*

♥ *Know what love is.*
   *True love can only be learned from God.*

♥ *See love the way God sees it.*
   *Love yourself.*
   *Value yourself.*
   *Be content where you are*
   *While you wait on the Lord.*
   *While you wait, occupy yourself,*
   *Go about your Father's business*
   *And fulfill your purpose on this earth.*

♥ *Looking back she often asked, who was that girl?*
   *So foolish*
   *Making such horrendous decisions.*
   *She became a girl so des-per-ate.*
   *She said some stupid things.*
   *She bared her soul and stooped low.*

♥ *Throughout this experience she learned that even Christian men play games.*

♥ *She is not a person who wants to play games.*
   *She learned that humans oftentimes change*
   *whom they are to become someone else in*
   *order to be liked or received.*

♥ *In the end she learned that being who she is at all times is best.*
 > *If she cannot be herself around a man he is definitely <u>NOT</u> the one.*

*Acknowledgements*

**To My Other Family and Friends...**
*Throughout my life I have met some wonderful people who have sown many seeds of greatness in me. Many of you I call friends are really my family. I love you all. Thanks for every word you have spoken in my life that gave me ideas, characters, inspiration, comfort and drive.*


***Courtney****, your eloquence amazes me.*
***Vicky****, thanks for believing not just in me, but the God in me.*
***Marlon****, thanks for believing in me.*
***Karen****, thanks for everything and thanks for your family*
***Benita****, I remembered when you said, "When are you going to write your book?"*
***Gillian****, thanks for your many prayers and thanks for listening.*
***Pauline Jean****, thanks for your encouragement. You were there when I wrestled with the decision to go back to school to pursue writing, since this was by no means on my radar to do in life, but God knows everything.*
***Ricardina "Coach Ricki"****...Thanks for how you inspire me, creatively.*
***Ms. Allen****, thanks for all the wisdom and principles you've given to me.*
***Deana****, thanks for your discernment.*
***Jaha****, your focus and determination has been a great inspiration to me, thanks.*

*Acknowledgements*

**Tara**, *your creativity and excitement is an inspiration.*
**Ms. Nancy**, *your life taught me to remain faithful to God no matter what.*
**Mr. James**, *your passion for God's word is an inspiration to me.*
**Ms. Midgette**, *how God has used you to help me believe in myself, Thanks!*

*A Big Thank You to:*

*My Immediate Family: The Richardson's and Nelson's,*
*My H.I.M. Family*
*My Children's Ministry Family,*
*My Drama Ministry Family,*
*My CCC Family,*
*My CAACS Family,*
*My Bamboo, Jamaica West Indies Family*

*To all the Professors at Brooklyn College who inspired me, but especially to Professors Burgess, McKay, Ames, Courtney, Phillips, Thomas and Bradshaw,*

*And so many others, too many to name...THANK YOU!!*

*Acknowledgements*

*Special Thanks to...*

**Pastor A. R. Bernard** *What can I say? From the first day I came to CCC I was enamored by the way you teach. For the first time in my life I was able to understand The Word. Everything you do is an encouragement to me. You never stop striving for progress and growth and success and for that I am thankful.*

**Pastor Karen Bernard** *Don't know if you remember the first day we met; it was when I came to interview for Children's Ministry. No one in a position like yours has ever made me feel so comfortable. Thank you!!*

*Acknowledgements*

*A Big Thank You:*

### To: Professor Matthew Burgess
### Brooklyn College

*Nervousness plagued my body the first day I entered.*
*You calmed my fears*
*Carefree Spirit*
*Wrapped up in wonderful layers*
*You are an offering to the world*
*Destined to impart*
*Fashioned to inspire and encourage*
*The sure*
*The unsure*
*You've left a seal on the fabric of*
*My soul*
*Permanently.*

*About The Poet*

*S**imple*
 *girl living in a complicated world*
*H**ow*
 *can she survive the forest?*
*E**agerly*
 *exuberant she treads the water*
*R**ising*
 *above the rough tide*
*Y**early*
 *progressing*
*L**earning...*

Sheryl Walcott graduated from Baruch College with a degree in Business Administration. She also graduated from Brooklyn College with a degree in Creative Writing. She is currently working to complete a Masters degree in Education. During her spare time, Ms. Walcott serves with her Missions team, H.I.M. (High Impact Missions), traveling to various countries around the world for Humanitarian and Evangelism purposes. She uses drama, poetry and her playwriting skills to bring what she calls HAIL (Hope, Awareness, Illumination and Love) to children, young people and adults globally.

Happiness; hopefulness; sorrow; pain; and yes, lust are the emotions that will be explored as you journey through the gifted poetry of Sheryl Walcott. Ultimately, God Is the True Love!!! But how do you deal with the emotional wants and needs of the heart? One-sided Love Affair will lay it all out while letting you know that you are not alone! ★ ★ ★ ★

- Susan D. Lord,
Playwright, Producer, Director, Author of *The Anointing*, *The Awakening, Be Careful of What You Ask For, Shadrach, Meshach and Abed-nego, With a Twist.*


This poet captures the insecurities, thoughts, and pain that I'm sure almost everyone has gone through at one time or another. I consider this to be a self-healing book for anyone who is striving for wholeness after suffering from the effects of a One-Sided Love Affair. I highly recommend this book for both men and women! ★ ★ ★ ★

-Robyn Traylor
Diversified Book Reviewer, .Com Entrepreneur,
Early Childhood Care Specialist, Business Manager,
and Marketing Consultant.

Printed by Libri Plureos GmbH in Hamburg, Germany